The Heritage Collection

The Extraordinary Educator: Dr. Delores Henderson

Rosemond Sarpong Owens
Illustrated by Amina Yakoob

Lion's Historian PRESS
Amplifying Authentic Voices

The Extraordinary Educator: Dr. Delores Henderson

Copyright ©2021 by Rosemond Sarpong Owens

Illustrator: Amina Yakoob

Editor: Sam Jones

All rights reserved.

No part of this publication may be reproduced, stored in a retrieval system, a database and/or published in any form or by any means, electronic, mechanical, photocopying, recording or otherwise, without the prior written permission of the publisher.

DEDICATION

This book is dedicated to
children in Minnesota.
Tap into your potential and realize it.
The sky is your limit!

CONTENTS

Chapter 1: A Star is Born 1

Chapter 2: Early Years 3

Chapter 3: Ohio's Finest 5

Chapter 4: The First of Many 7

Chapter 5: A Force For Education 9

Chapter 6: Family is Everything 11

Chapter 7: Principal Delores 13

Chapter 8: The Power of One 15

Chapter 9: Retirement – Not Her Thing 17

Chapter 10: An All Time Legend 19

References 21

About the Author 22

Acknowledgements 23

Chapter 1

A Star is Born

On a beautiful day in Carrollton, Ohio, Maudie and Leila Williams welcomed into the world a daughter, Delores. What a beautiful sight to behold. Baby Delores warmed the hearts of everyone who saw her. Family members wondered how a child so small could bring so much joy.

Chapter 2
Early Years

Delores grew up on a small farm with chickens and pigs, and she loved to play outdoors with her many siblings. She also enjoyed learning. From an early age, Maudie and Leila knew Delores was very smart and destined for greatness. At six years of age, because Delores excelled in her studies, she skipped kindergarten and first grade, joining second graders at the Waynesburg Elementary School. Delores treasured reading time, going everywhere carrying a book.

Chapter 3

Ohio's Finest

During high school, Delores played the clarinet, as she continued to excel in school. She adored her eldest sister, Ella, who was the valedictorian of her graduating high school class. It was sad in those days because there was a lot of racism. Ella, because she was an African American in a rural white area, was not permitted to claim her rightful place as valedictorian and speak to her graduating classmates. Delores admired Ella's courage, who rose above the difficult rural conditions and vowed to follow in her eldest sister's footsteps. Soon, Delores graduated from Sandy Valley High School at age fifteen, several years younger than her peers.

Chapter 4
The First of Many

After high school, Delores enrolled at the Wilberforce University, a Historically Black College. Here, she continued to excel in her studies and participated in many extra-curricular activities. In 1961, Delores, still passionate about the clarinet played at the Madison Square Garden in New York City. What an honor and a privilege for Delores! While at college, she also became a member of the Delta Sigma Theta Sorority, Incorporated. Delores completed her bachelor of science in education program at Wilberforce University in three years.

Chapter 5
A Force For Education

Delores got a taste for teaching during her first experience as an educator in Ohio's Springfield School system. While in Ohio, Delores's beloved Roy, who was her high school sweetheart, proposed over the phone. After a year in Ohio, Delores moved to the Midwest state of Minnesota, where she and Roy Henderson got married.

In Minnesota, Delores took up a position in the St. Paul School District and never looked back. As a teacher, she saw potential in every child and made it her duty to tell each child that they were special. Delores believed in the children who were in her school. Delores spoke positively into children's lives. She was persistent until they were convinced of the potential they carried. Delores made St. Paul her home and contributed in every way possible to improve the lives of children in Minnesota.

Delores also continued with her own studies in education administration at the University of Minnesota, becoming Dr. Henderson in 1982. Delores also received an honorary Doctorate of Human Letters from Macalester College in St. Paul.

Chapter 6
Family is Everything

Delores grew up in a loving family on the small farm in Ohio and appreciated the value it added to her life. Delores, in turn, built a beautiful family life with sweetheart Roy, adding Mercedes to the family. Mercedes was a source of pride and joy. Mercedes grew up with adoring parents who were committed to giving back to their community. They taught Mercedes at an early age to give back too. Today, Mercedes is a leader in her own right and supports the work of Dr. Henderson, along with her husband Eric Clark.

Chapter 7
Principal Delores

Delores has been a longtime advocate for children. Whether as a teacher or a principal, Delores was the voice of children for change and improved opportunities for excellence in education. Delores served as an assistant superintendent with South St. Paul Public Schools.

Chapter 8

The Power of One

Many of us wonder how much difference we can make as individuals. Dr. Henderson's life demonstrates that a single person can accomplish a lot. Dr. Henderson served as an administrator in the St. Paul Public School System for many years. During this time, she developed and sustained the Gifted and Talented Magnet, formerly J.J. Hill Gifted and Talented, now known as Capitol Hill. She was also a pioneer in the desegregation of Eastside and Westside schools.

In addition, Dr. Henderson has served as an instructor at Hamline University, Metropolitan State University, and the University of Minnesota. Dr. Henderson remains an active alumna of Wilberforce University and the University of Minnesota. Her husband, Roy, until his passing, cheered Delores on, and celebrated her many accomplishments.

Chapter 9
Retirement – Not Her Thing

What does retirement mean for Dr. Henderson? I think we can look at retirement in a new way through her life. She is a retired school principal; however, she is not retired from the work. Dr. Henderson remains busy as ever. She continues to mentor young people and anyone who comes her way. Dr. Henderson is a visionary who created the path for a more just and equitable education system.

Recently, Dr. Henderson established a new non-profit to support education, **D.E.L.O.R.E.S. WORKS, Incorporated**. The mission is to assist in closing achievement and opportunity gaps for under-represented middle school students. The end goal is to empower students to attain their full potential and become members of a global society.

Chapter 10
An All Time Legend

Wherever Dr. Henderson finds herself, she meets many who were either former students, or teaching colleagues. Dr. Henderson's love for children and teaching influenced the transformational changes she made to educational practices in the state of Minnesota. These changes were critical toward improving educational experiences of children of color.

In acknowledgement of Dr. Henderson's contribution to education, she has received awards too numerous to name. For example, the Minnesota National Principal of the Year and Martin Luther King, Jr. Education Awards. She served on many boards: Regions Hospital, United Hospital, the University of Minnesota Fairview Hospitals, St. John's University Board of Regents, Cretin-Derham High School, and Catholic Charities Boards. In addition, Dr. Henderson is associated with various local and international organizations: Minneapolis-St. Paul Chapter of Delta Sigma Theta Sorority, Inc., where she is a charter member, and the Minneapolis-St. Paul Chapter of the Links, Inc., the longest serving Central Area Director.

REFERENCES

1. Moore Crosby Meredith, " Dr. Delores Henderson exemplifies the 'power of one' Insight News, June 26th, 2017, Updated, April 11th, 2018.

2. Verges Josh, "St. Paul principal wins racial equity leadership award", Pioneer Press, November 1st, 2014, Updated, October 28th, 2015.

ABOUT THE AUTHOR

Rosemond Sarpong Owens is a diversity, equity & inclusion professional. She has a passion for history and storytelling and is inspired to share stories of heroes and heroines of African descent.

Sarpong Owens is a wife and mother to three girls who love to read. She hopes that this book encourages children to be proud of themselves and their heritage.

ACKNOWLEDGEMENTS

For providing content and support,
thanks to Mercedes Henderson-Clark.

For assistance with copyediting,
thanks to Letitia deGraft Okyere.

For support and guidance,
thanks to Marjy Marj (Marjorie Boafo Appiah).

For formatting and design,
thanks to Nasim Malik Sarkar.

www.ingramcontent.com/pod-product-compliance
Lightning Source LLC
Chambersburg PA
CBHW041707160426
43209CB00017B/1765